YOU
And Your Body
BOOK B

SCHOLASTIC INC.

Senior Vice President, Director of Education: Dr. Ernest Fleishman
Editor in Chief: Catherine Vanderhoof
Managing Editor: Sandy Kelley
Writers: Katherine-Kerry L. Bozza and Jessica Cherry
Vice President, Director, Editorial Design and Production:
Will Kefauver
Art Director: Joan Michael
Designer: Lillie Caporlingua, Bill SMITH STUDIO
Cover Design: Joan Michael
Cover Photo: Bill Westheimer
Illustrators: Kate Flanagan, Bernard Adnet, Jennifer Bruce
Assistant Production Director: Bryan Samolinski

The information and activities that comprise this series are largely
based on the KNOW YOUR BODY (KYB) Comprehensive
School Health Promotion Program.

For additional information about the KNOW YOUR BODY
program, contact the American Health Foundation at
(212) 953-1900.

Contents

Eat Smart

Your body needs lots of different foods to grow up big and strong. That is why you need to "eat smart" when you choose foods. Eating too much fat and sugar is bad for your heart and teeth. Use these lights to help you remember how to eat smart.

A green light means "go." GO foods are good for your heart. It is OK to GO ahead and eat them anytime you are hungry. Here are some GO foods:

A yellow light means "go slow or be careful." THINK foods are second best. Before you eat a THINK food, stop and think, "Can I eat any GO foods instead?" If not, go ahead and enjoy these foods. Here are some THINK foods:

A red light means "stop." STOP foods are not-so-healthy foods that are high in fat or sugar. You should try to eat these foods only once in a while. Here are some STOP foods:

5

Lunch Choices

Juanita needs to pack her lunch. But she can't decide between the foods in the refrigerator. Circle some GO foods you think Juanita should choose. Draw Juanita's healthy lunch in the lunchbag.

6

Smart Shopping

Robert has a list of foods to buy at the store. The store has three aisles. Aisle #1 has only **GO** foods. Aisle #2 has only **THINK** foods. And Aisle #3 has only **STOP** foods on its shelves. Help Robert figure out where to find each item on his list.

SHOPPING LIST   AISLE #

Brown rice _____
Peanut butter _____
Chocolate bars _____
Soda pop _____
Cream cheese _____
Ham _____
Skinless chicken _____
Swiss cheese _____
Potatoes _____
Fruit juice _____

Breakfast Record

It is important to start every day with a healthy breakfast. Breakfast gives you energy to get through the day and helps you think better at school.

Make a list of what you eat for breakfast every day for a week.

Monday	
Tuesday	
Wednesday	
Thursday	
Friday	

Circle the **GO** foods in green.
Circle the **THINK** foods in yellow.
Circle the **STOP** foods in red.

What are some GO breakfast foods you could eat instead of the STOP foods?

_____

Tooth Talk

How Well Do You Know Your Teeth?

You have 20 baby teeth. Your baby teeth fall out to make room for 32 new teeth. You will keep these teeth for the rest of your life if you take good care of them.

The picture below shows a grown-up's mouth and what the different kinds of teeth do:

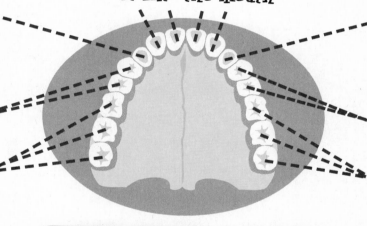

Incisors (8)
✓ Cut food and help guide it into the mouth

Canines (4)
✓ Grasp and tear food

Premolars (8)
✓ Crush and tear food

Molars (12)
✓ Chew and grind food

Canines (4)
✓ Grasp and tear food

Premolars (8)
✓ Crush and tear food

Molars (12)
✓ Chew and grind food

Tooth Tips

✓ Brush your teeth three times a day.
✓ Use a toothbrush with soft, even bristles.
✓ Use a toothpaste with fluoride.
✓ Visit a dentist at least once a year.
✓ Ask an adult to help floss between your teeth.
✓ Eat healthy tooth snacks like fresh vegetables and fruits instead of sugary foods like cakes and cookies.
✓ Brush soon after you eat, especially after you eat sugary foods.

Plaque Attack

Plaque is a clear, sticky layer of germs on your teeth. Plaque can cause lots of trouble (like cavities, or holes in your teeth). By brushing every day, you can help get rid of plaque.

Name the plaque-fighters in this picture.

t _ _ _ _ _ b _ _ _ _ _   t _ _ _ _ p _ _ _ _ _

d _ _ _ _ _ _ f _ _ _ _   d _ _ _ _ _ _ t

Win's Winning Smile

Win has a winning smile. Circle what Win does to keep her teeth healthy.

1. Win brushes   I   3   times a day.

2. This is Win's toothpaste:

3. Win eats    as a snack.

4. This is Win playing hockey:

Tooth Trail

Find your way through the maze. Draw a path that
leads to a winning smile and healthy teeth.

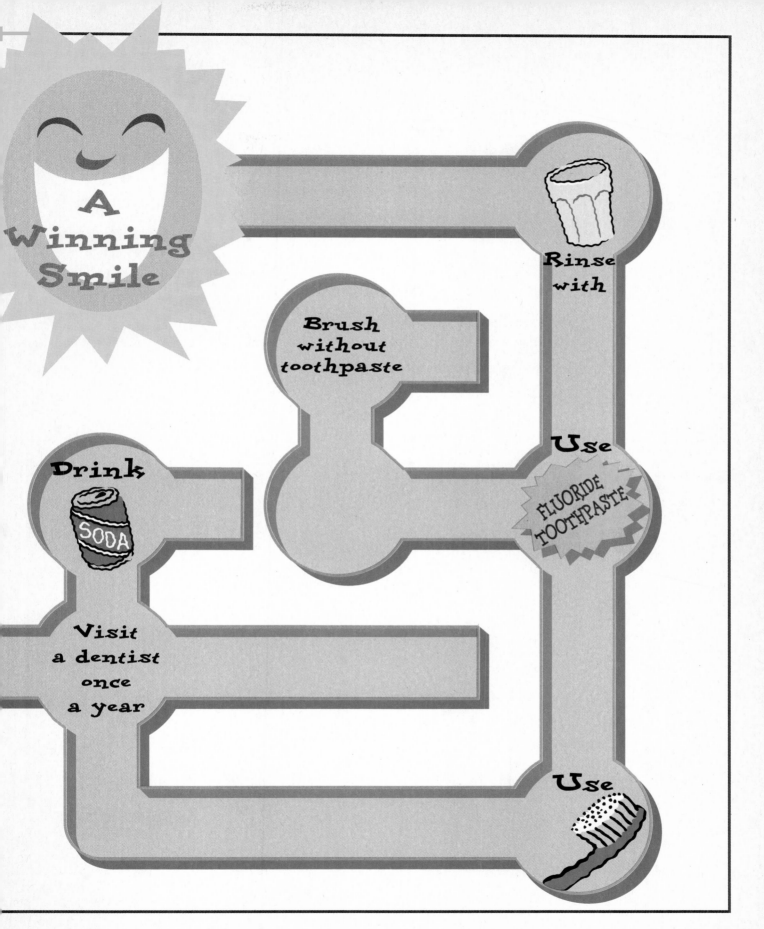

A Winning Smile

Rinse with

Brush without toothpaste

Use FLUORIDE TOOTHPASTE

Drink SODA

Visit a dentist once a year

Use

Exercise Wise

When you run and play, you are keeping fit. Exercise can help your body, especially your heart.

Heart-healthy exercises make you huff and puff. Your heart beats faster, and you breathe more quickly. You should do heart-healthy exercise for about 15-30 minutes at a time. Here are some examples of heart-healthy exercises:

In-line skating

Playing tag

Biking

Walking quickly

Cross-country skiing

Jumping rope

Swimming

The Path to Fitness

Fill in the missing letters to find the mystery words below.

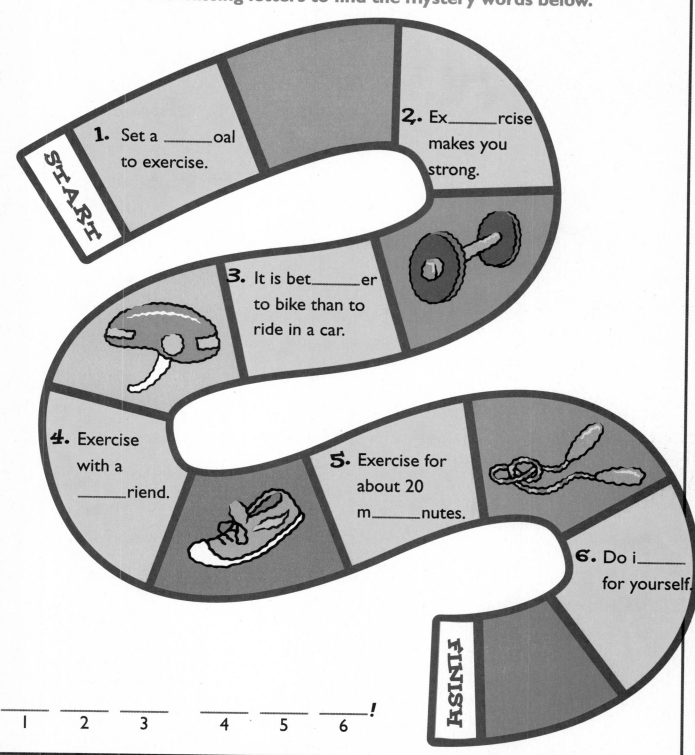

START

1. Set a _____ oal to exercise.

2. Ex _____ rcise makes you strong.

3. It is bet _____ er to bike than to ride in a car.

4. Exercise with a _____ riend.

5. Exercise for about 20 m _____ nutes.

6. Do i _____ for yourself.

FINISH

_____ _____ _____ _____ _____ _____ !
1   2   3   4   5   6

At the Park

Circle each person doing a heart-healthy exercise.

Safety Smart

Here are some ways to stay safe.

Keeping Safe at Home

Be safety smart when you are at home. Do not touch or play with:

- ✓ sharp things, like knives, scissors, needles, glass, or razor blades
- ✓ plastic bags
- ✓ hot stoves
- ✓ fire, such as matches, candles, or lighters

Make sure you and your family have a fire escape plan. Then you will know what to do and where to go if there is a fire in your home.

Keeping Safe Outside

- ✓ Play away from the street and parked cars.
- ✓ Do not follow your ball into the street.
- ✓ Be careful on slides and swings.
- ✓ Look and listen before you cross the street.
- ✓ Always wear your seat belt when you are in a car.

If You Need Help

Keep numbers for the fire station, police station, and doctor near the telephone. Make sure you know of one grown-up that you can go to if you need help.

In an Emergency, Dial 911

Say **WHO** you are:

NAME: _____

Say **WHERE** you are:

ADDRESS: _____

_____

TELEPHONE #: _____

TELL WHAT HAPPENED

Don't hang up until the person on the other end says it's OK!!

Check It Out

In this kitchen, there are five home safety hazards. Can you find them? Cross out each hazard that you see. There are three things that could help in an emergency. Circle them.

The Meaning of Prevention

Put a check ☑ next to the picture in each set that best shows the meaning of *prevention*.

How I Stay Safe

There are many things you can do to stay safe, like wearing a seat belt in a car or not playing with matches. Draw a picture of something you do in order to stay safe and healthy.

The Safe Way to Go

Using the key, choose the safest path to get to the playground.

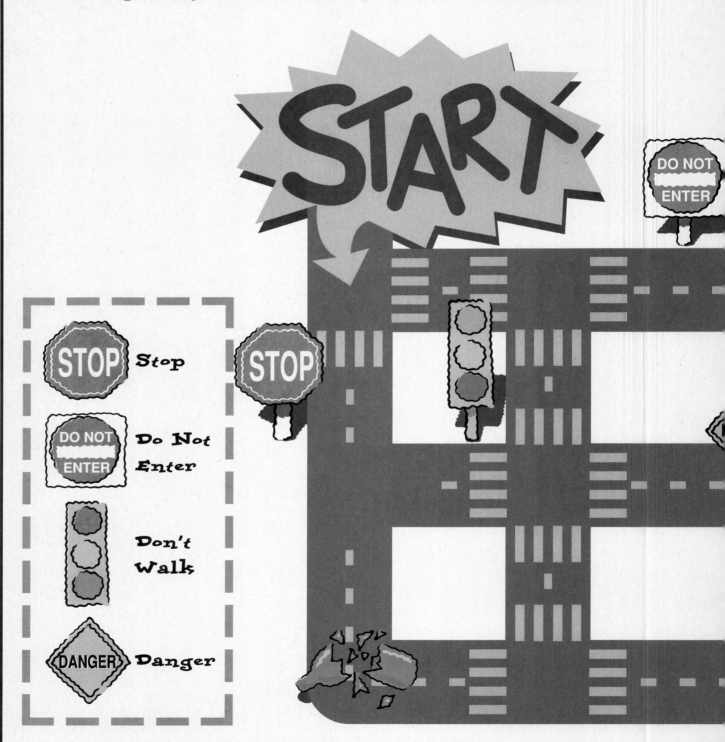

Watch Me Grow

All children are different from each other in some ways.

You and your friends may also be alike in some ways.
Can you name two ways that you and your friends are alike?

_____

_____

As you grow older, your body will change.
The jobs and things you can do change too.

Some of the things you can do now might be:

Some things you may be able to do when you are older are:

Are We the Same or Different?

There are many different types of animals. Some animals have two feet, and some have four. Some have hair and some do not. People are different too. But are people and animals alike? What animals look like you? Let's find out. Answer these questions about the animals below.

bird   monkey   child   elephant   dog

Which walk on two legs?———————————————————

Which eat peanuts?————————————————————

Which have a tail?—————————————————————

Which have ears?—————————————————————

Draw your favorite animal.
How is this animal like you?

————————————————

How is it different?

————————————————

As You Grow

Your needs change as you grow older. Look at the chart below. Put a check in the boxes under the baby for each thing a baby needs. Put a check in the second column for each thing you need now. Put a check in the third column for each thing you will need when you are older.

sleep			
clothes			
love			
measles shots			
books			
car seat			
diapers			
friends			
school			
milk			
parents			
food			
help			
smile			

Look at You Now!

On the chart, check all the things you can do.
Then draw a picture of yourself doing something you
like to do.

wash my hair	
make my bed	
feed my pet	
talk to a friend	
give someone a hug	
play a game	
tie my shoes	
drive a car	
ride a bike	
swim	
clean my room	

Compare your chart with charts done by your friends.
Do you do things that are the same?

Friends and Family

We need to get along with many different people — with our friends, our family, our classmates, and our teachers.

Here are things you can do to get along with others:

- ✓ be honest
- ✓ be polite
- ✓ be a good listener
- ✓ share
- ✓ respect other people's points of view

Friendship

Use the code below to figure out these words that tell about friendship.

A	B	C	D	E	F	G	H	I	J	K	L	M
24	25	26	1	2	3	4	5	6	7	8	9	10

N	O	P	Q	R	S	T	U	V	W	X	Y	Z
11	12	13	14	15	16	17	18	19	20	21	22	23

5 12 11 2 16 17 _____

13 12 9 6 17 2 _____

3 15 6 2 11 1 9 22 _____

What words would you pick to tell about friendship? Use the code to spell them. Then see if your friends can solve them.

I Am Special

Put each one of your fingers on an ink pad. Then place your fingerprints in the correct spaces below.

Thumb	1st finger	2nd finger	3rd finger	4th finger

Look at your fingerprints. Look at your classmates' fingerprints. Are they the same or different?

_____

Write a poem about yourself that tells what makes you special.

Families

Every family is special, because no two families are exactly alike.

Robinson lives with his mother and his father.

Ingrid lives with her mother and father, 3 brothers, her aunt, her grandmother, and her great-grandfather.

David lives with his father and his sister.

What kind of a family do you have? Draw a picture of your family.

What is something that your family likes to do together?

_____

37

Working It Out

We all have conflicts with others.

Each of these pictures shows a conflict.
How would you solve the problem?

Situation 1

It's my turn!

Answer: _____

_____

_____

Situation 2

You can't wear that shirt—it looks terrible!

But it's my favorite!

Answer: _____

_____

_____

Germ-Free Me

Germs are things that can make you sick. Germs can enter your body through your mouth and your nose, and through cuts on your skin that are not covered up with a bandage.

Germs can be passed when people sneeze or cough, or share things like combs, toothbrushes, and cups. Germs can cause diseases like a cold, the chicken pox, or measles.

Not all diseases come from germs. Sometimes people are born with diseases or disabilities.

39

What Am I?

There are many things that can help you stay healthy and germ free. Match the pictures on the right with the correct description on the left to find out what some of these things are.

I have teeth.
I keep your hair neat.
I am a _____.

I am long and thin.
I help to keep your mouth clean.
I am a _____.

I am used to cover your mouth
and nose when you sneeze.
I am made of paper.
I am a _____.

I make your hands clean.
I am used before you eat.
I am _____.

40

Keep Germs Away

Cross out the pictures that show how germs can enter your body.

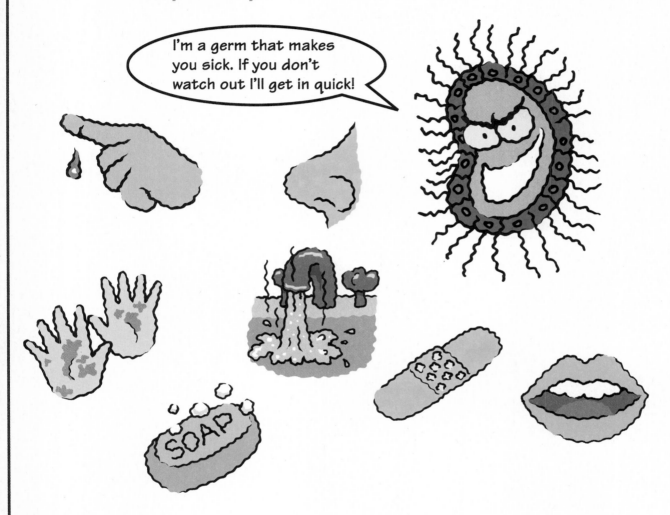

Now on the lines, write the names of the pictures that are left. They will help to keep germs away.

We're _____, _____ and _____.

We'll stop germs quick.
We watch out, so you don't get sick!

Fighting Germs

Your body fights germs in lots of different ways. But your body needs your help! Is each child helping to keep his or her body strong to fight germs? Check yes or no. If you checked no, write a sentence to tell what that child should do instead.

MiWon goes to the doctor for her checkup and shots.

☐ yes ☐ no

_____

_____

_____

- -

Tyrone chews on his pencil to help him think.

☐ yes ☐ no

_____

_____

_____

Emily likes to stay up late to watch TV.

☐ yes ☐ no

_____

_____

- - - - - - - - - - - - - - - - - -

José eats a healthy breakfast.

☐ yes ☐ no

_____

_____

- - - - - - - - - - - - - - - - - -

Anita is in too much of a hurry to use soap.

☐ yes ☐ no

_____

_____

- - - - - - - - - - - - - - - - - -

Dave gets exercise every day.

☐ yes ☐ no

_____

_____

Secret to Good Health!

Add and subtract letters to form a secret message. Place the words in the correct spaces below to find out what the message is.

1. know - kw + brush - rush + floss - flss + body - bo =

_____

2. teeth - eeth + make - m + ears - ear =

_____

3. book - ook + feet - fe + stress - srss + run - un =

_____

4. carrot - rot + ear - ar =

_____

5. look - lok + fast - ast =

_____

6. healthy - health + go - g + uncle - ncle =

_____

7. sit - si + hand - d =

_____

8. yes - es + mouth - mth

_____

_____ _____ _____ _____ _____ _____ _____ _____
  1   2   3   4   5   6   7   8

Healthy Choices

You eat and drink food to stay healthy and strong. You eat and drink medicine from a doctor to get better when you are sick. But not everything is safe to eat, drink, or breathe.

Poisons

Poisons can make us very sick or even kill us. Many things that we use to clean the floor, windows, and even our clothes can hurt us if we eat or drink them. Some are even dangerous to smell.

Medicine

Medicine can help you feel better when you are sick, but it can hurt you if not taken the way a doctor says. You should never take medicine from strangers or from other children.

Alcohol

Beer and other drinks that grown-ups sometimes drink can be very dangerous for children. They contain a drug called *alcohol*.

Smoke

Smoke from cigarettes can hurt you if you breathe it in. Smoke makes it harder for your body to work right.

You can keep yourself safe
from all *these* things.
Can you *think* how?

What Would You Do?

Sometimes you have to make decisions about your health. Write what you would do or say.

You are playing at your friend's house. Your friend's teenage brother is in the kitchen smoking with some friends. They ask if you want to try. What could you do or say?

_____

_____

_____

- - - - - - - - - - - - - - - - - - - -

You are at a big family barbecue. Some of your cousins are looking for beer cans with beer left in them so they can drink it. What could you do or say?

_____

_____

_____

You are waiting for your parent on the school playground with one of your friends. A stranger asks you if you want some candy. What could you do or say?

_____

_____

_____

- - - - - - - - - - - - - - - - - - -

Your friend found some pills at home and brought them to school. At recess she wants you to try them with her. What could you do or say?

_____

_____

_____

Be Smart, Don't Start!

How would you tell other kids about the dangers of smoking or using drugs? You could make a poster. You could make a button, T-shirt, or bumper sticker. You could create a rhyme or rap song. Use the space below to create your special message.